The Little Book of
INTROVERTED
THOUGHTS

Talisha A. Matheson

© 2023 The Inspired Introvert
All Rights Reserved

ISBN: 978-1-7777453-3-2

Disclaimer: These quotes are the intellectual property taken from published and unpublished works of The Inspired Introvert. All other quotes are credited to the best of my knowledge.

Dear Reader,

*The Little Book Of Introverted Thoughts
is a collection of random musings
and encouragement. No matter where
you are, I hope you find some inspiration
between these pages and let the
message permeate the corners
of your mind.*

Be Inspired!

Why do we crave to be a *priority* in someone's life while taking the *back seat* in ours?

When we desire to *understand* others, beautiful things *transpire*.

Shame
is its own
form of
confinement!

You can't move beyond the *hurt* if you keep sitting in the *midst* of it.

Admitting that you are in *need* is one of the most *powerful* acts of maturity and vulnerability.

We can't be *everything* to everyone and *nothing* to ourselves.

Treat *victory* and *defeat* the same because they are both *temporary.*

— Tim Ross

Having a *new* way of *thinking* makes you deliberate in how you *live* your life.

Nothing is worse than *pouring* **into a cup with a** *hole.*

Find *someone* you can love without losing *yourself.*

Be easy to *love*
and *hard* **to forget.**

— *Unknown*

Love *firmly*,
profoundly and
intentionally
so they never
question
your *sincerity*.

The curator of *negative* words has a short memory, but the receiver always *remembers.*

Seek *balance* between the loudness of your *mind* and the whisper of your *heart.*

Don't be so love-shy that you harden *tender* moments with *memories* of hurt.

When the *softer* side of you has found a *place* to call home, you will like it there. You will be *comfortable* enough to kick off your shoes and lay your head down and rest; THIS is where you *belong.*

Sometimes, unwavering *strength* and independence are rooted in old pain, falsely *protecting* us from a hurt that may never show its *face*.

We *live*
in a world
with instant
gratification
and delayed
thankfulness.

Value yourself more than you *expect* value from others.

Just because *you* want it doesn't mean it will want you *back*, and the latter doesn't decrease your *worth*.

We all have *limitations,* and we need to be *willing* to rely on others.

Being forever *strong* is exhausting. It's okay to be *soft* and pliable.

You are not for *everyone,* and everyone is *not* for *you.*

Be *intentional*
in everything
you *say* and *do.*

No one can *undo* what God has *purposed* for every corner of your *life.*

Acknowledge the *intricate* parts of a kind *gesture* and not the result.

Remember,
when your enough
doesn't *feel*
like enough,
you are *enough!*

Vulnerability requires *trust* and *respect*, and when either is *fractured*, we can't expect it to willingly *show* its face.

As much as we want to be on the *receiving* end of life-filled words, how often are we the *authors* of them?

You can't
force others
to *see* you
if you don't
see *yourself.*

Rest is not
a luxury.
It's a *right!*

When you set *boundaries,* the ones who are *most* upset are those who *benefited* from your lack.

Rest *opens* **the gateway to** *peace.*

Never *adjust*
who you are
to fit into a *mould*,
that was
never *designed*
for you.

Why can we find the *strength* to encourage others but not *ourselves?*

Overthinking is a *mental* bully.

Thoughts are *seeds*, and the mind is *soil*. What we think *grows*.

Never give *people* access to you if you have to *recover* from them upon their *departure.*

Be open
to *sharing*
your time,
and be *careful*
not to waste it.

Distractions will *interfere* with your identity if you don't know *who* you are, *why* you are, *where* you are or where you're *going*.

Silence **can be both bondage and** *freedom.*

Not everyone has the *capacity* to receive the love you *give.*

Hearts that
have experienced
hurt and
then healed
love harder.

Wounded **minds that renew think** *deeper* **than those who don't.**

Bitterness
is like cancer.
It eats upon
the host,
but anger
is like fire.
It burns it
all *clean.*

— Maya Angelou

You can't freely *love* until you *forgive.*

Sometimes, the *ultimate* form of intimacy is sitting in *silence*.

Your desire to *change* needs to be *stronger* than your desire to *remain* the same.

— Unknown

Don't let
the scars
of *yesterday*
make you
rigid *today.*

Taste and *digest* your words *before* you speak them.

Don't be so *committed to* failure that you never *try* again.

**If we have
to** *chase*
**something,
it doesn't want
to be** *caught.*

Are you *doing* the *right* thing by doing nothing?

The only things we can *control* in life are the *choices* we make.

Judgements expose *character*.

Souls **don't merely meet.**
They *recognize.*

The *love*
you give
mimics the love
you have
for *yourself.*

Happiness is a *feeling* that comes and goes; *fulfillment* lasts forever.

— *Unknown*

Vulnerability breathes life into *relationships.* Its absence cuts off its *air* supply.

Slow down; anything worth *having* takes time and *patience.*

If we spend more time *being kind*, uplifting, and less critical, the *world* will look different.

Nothing you ever go through is *wasted.*

— Tim Ross

In our *desire* to constantly *protect* others, we often leave ourselves *exposed.*

Romance **is the low-hanging** *fruit* **of the experience of** *love.*

— Karega Bailey

What we *tell* ourselves alters who we *become*.

Healing **requires us to** *acknowledge* **the pain we have caused** *others.*

We fear the *familiar* ache of a broken heart, but no *matter* its severity, *brokenness* is always followed by *healing*.

What we say is *important,* and why we say it is *essential.* How we say it is *paramount.*

**Relationships
are** *simple.*
**The people in them
are** *complicated.*

Seek to *understand* **so you can be** *understood.*

— Tony Gaskins

Consistency is the cement that keeps *relationships* together.

Failure **doesn't mean all is lost. Sometimes more is** *learned* **from failure than from** *success.*

— Tim Ross

If they *know* everything about us and we know *nothing* about them, *perhaps* we talk more than we *listen.*

Relationships can fall into two categories, divine *connections* or destructive *distractions.*

— Unknown

Do not *unearth* things
you planted
in *faith*.
Leave it there
and allow it
to *grow*.

— Jerry Flowers Jr

Stop *normalizing* dysfunction. Just because you're used to it doesn't mean it's *healthy*.

We can either *grow* by what we go *through* or remain stuck.

Being *comfortable* **in your dysfunction is** *imprisonment.*

Your *value* doesn't decrease based on someone's inability to see your *worth*.

Being on the *journey* **is just as important as its** *purpose.*

True *character* is dictated by how you *treat* people when life isn't going your *way*.

Remove **who and what doesn't help you** *evolve.*

Do what sets your *soul* on fire.

The *truth* isn't popular, so we are *comforted* by lies.

When love *knocks* on your door, don't let *fear* make you act like you are *not* home.

Emotional *triggers* will expose two things — *unhealed* parts of us or *toxic* parts of them.

Sometimes, we *break* our hearts by having unrealistic *expectations* of others.

Those who *dare* to speak the *truth* also dare to face it, no *matter* how painful or disappointing it might be.

The *choices* **you make do** *not* **have to** *make sense* **to everyone.**

Always
love from
the *right* place
for the right
reasons.

We've become so *comfortable* with counterfeits that we no longer recognize *authenticity.*

Surviving
**is important.
Thriving is**
elegant.

— Maya Angelou

A tree's *strength* is not determined by its branches' height but by its *roots'* depth.

Find, *keep* and *nurture* the ones who choose to *love* us *despite* our messiest *seasons.*

Consistency is *discipline* on repeat.

— *Jerry Flowers Jr*

Refrain from thinking so far into the *future* that you forget to *live* today.

You can't build with *someone* who refuses to do the heavy *lifting.* You can't grow with them if they refuse to *see* your *need* for water.

— Unknown

What *you* do
is not as
important as
who *you* are.

Many prefer the *surface* over the deep because *depth* requires the *truth.*

Don't judge each *day* by the harvest you reap but by the *seeds* that you plant.

— Robert Louis Stevenson

Being placed in a box and *choosing* to remain there are two *different* things.

Never **give so** *much* **of yourself that** *you* **no longer** *exist.*

We can't *have a future* if we refuse to do the *work* in the *present.*

The *purest* love is one you *give* freely, expecting *nothing* in *return*.

*Also by Talisha A Matheson
Soul Talks: 52-Weeks of Inspiration*

www.ingramcontent.com/pod-product-compliance
Lightning Source LLC
Chambersburg PA
CBHW030042100526
44590CB00011B/299